BANKRL
EXPLAI

The Bankruptcy Association's
Practical Guide to UK Insolvency Laws

BANKRUPTCY EXPLAINED

The Bankruptcy Association's Practical Guide to UK Insolvency Laws

John McQueen

The Bankruptcy Association
of Great Britain and Ireland

THIS BOOK IS A PUBLICATION OF

The Bankruptcy Association
of Great Britain and Ireland

4 Johnson Close
Abraham Heights
Lancaster
Lancashire
LA1 5EU
United Kingdom
Tel: (01524) 64305

First edition: October 1995
Reprinted: October 1998

Conditions of Sale

Great efforts have been made by the Publisher and Author to ensure
that information contained in this book is accurate. Information can
become out of date, however, and errors can creep in because of author's
and printer's errors. This book is sold, therefore, on the condition that
neither Author nor Publisher can be held legally responsible for the
consequence of any error or omission there may be.

ISBN 0 9518636 5 7

Printed and bound in Great Britain by
Redwood Books, Trowbridge, Wiltshire

Phototypeset by Intype, London

Contents

If you lived in the richest, most powerful city it was possible for a man to imagine, but there was no love there, no mercy and no justice for those who met with misfortune; then you would be better off dead than to live in such a place.

Foreword

I founded the Bankruptcy Association of Great Britain and Ireland more than 12 years ago, during March 1983. Since then I have spent most of my time living and breathing bankruptcy law and surrounding issues. During this period I have advised at least 10,000 individuals on their bankruptcy problems. Currently I am advising about 1,500 bankrupt people each year.

Knowledge and experience gained during this period is presented in this book, in a condensed form, in order to help those people who are experiencing bankruptcy, as well as their advisers. It covers the law in every country in the United Kingdom. The law in England, Wales and Northern Ireland is the same, but there are some important differences in the law in Scotland.

Bankruptcy is a much misunderstood subject. Few people study the subject properly, added to which there are also many grey areas of the law. As a result, many professional advisers, such as accountants, solicitors and advice agencies, are often woefully inadequate in the advice they offer people.

The facts presented in this book regarding the law in the United Kingdom (excluding Scotland) have been checked by two specialist lawyers, Christopher Garwood and Andrew Laycock, from Carrick Read Insolvency. Chapter 8, which covers the law in Scotland, has been checked by Alan O'Boyle, a Scottish insolvency practitioner. I should like to thank these three gentlemen for their time and the help they have provided.

I must also thank Gill Hankey, who not only runs the Bankruptcy Association with me, but who has also acted as editor-in-chief of this book. Editing a book is often much harder work than writing it and I am grateful for the effort Gill has put into it.

The opinions expressed in this book are, however, entirely my own. I would also comment that the law is a 'strange mistress.' This book attempts to explain complex technical legislation in simple English. It is in the nature of such an undertaking that some of the 'ifs and buts' of the law will be glossed over, or simply not covered, on the grounds that they rarely arise or present a problem. The main strength of this book is that the writer has been involved daily in advising on bankruptcy matters for more than a decade. I am therefore aware of the main practical queries which people raise. I am confident that I have dealt with the vast majority of these.

I hope this book will be a useful guide for people regarding bankruptcy law. This book is based on my understanding of the law as it stands at 21 July 1995.

It has been my great privilege to serve the bankrupt community of the United Kingdom for more than a decade. I dedicate this book to all the brave men and women who suffer the indignities of bankruptcy each year.

John McQueen
Lancaster
20 September 1995

1

Setting the Scene

I need to paint a big scene in this chapter because most people entering a bankruptcy scenario for the first time lack any knowledge of the subject and are frightened and intimidated about the prospect. The biggest and most important thing I can do for such people is to show them the whole picture. This will then help each individual to find their own personal perspective on their problems.

Since 1990, many tens of thousands of people have gone into bankruptcy each year, due to the collapse of the property market and the terrible economic slump which followed. These people come from every walk of life. There is really no such thing as a typical bankrupt, although if I had to pluck one out of the air he might be a fifty year old graduate, running his own business, with a wife and three teenage children to support. Bankruptcy may well shatter such a person's life.

Most people who go bankrupt do so due to debts accrued whilst running a business. Other people go bankrupt because of mortgage shortfalls arising on repossessed homes, others on credit card debts. An increasing number of students are also going bankrupt as they leave university with loans and borrowings they cannot service.

The difficult economic circumstances currently facing the people

1

of Britain are forcing more and more people to form their own businesses, simply because there are not enough 'real' jobs available. As a result, the surge of bankruptcies which began in 1990 is likely to continue, at least until the end of this century and possibly forever.

There is perhaps one chance in a hundred of a new venture surviving more than ten years – such are the difficulties of founding and running a successful company. Any new business faces hundreds of problems and these ensure that most will fail. This is a sad fact of British commercial life.

I founded the Bankruptcy Association in 1983 after my eldest brother, Jim, a builder went bankrupt for a second time. He had first gone bankrupt as a young man, recovered from that bankruptcy, and then went bankrupt again 20 years later, due to tax debts. I feel sure that the pressures he came under contributed to his early death in 1989, when he was just 48 years old. I had also experienced horrendous debt problems myself after going to university as a mature student, whilst I had a wife and three young sons to support. My involvement, therefore, is close and personal. I know how it feels to be burdened and humiliated with debt problems.

When I first became involved in the bankruptcy scene it seemed a shadowy, twilight world and must seem so to many who first approach it now. Thanks to my experiences within this strange world, I can at least shine a bright spotlight on it to help others.

Bankruptcies are currently administered by the Insolvency Service, an executive agency of the Department of Trade and Industry. About 2,000 people administer their headquarters and staff a chain of about forty official receivers' offices around England, Wales and Northern Ireland. The official receiver is the Insolvency Service official in charge of each district and it is at this level that bankrupt people first come into contact with the Insolvency Service. There are government proposals being discussed at the moment which may lead to many of the functions of the Insolvency Service being privatised and placed in the hands of firms of insolvency practitioners or some other organisations.

Insolvency practitioners are mainly accountants, who are qualified and authorised to administer the affairs of individual bankrupts. When a person goes bankrupt, if he has assets, an insolvency practitioner is appointed as trustee in bankruptcy, to dispose of these assets. If there are no assets and therefore no fees to pay a private insolvency practitioner, then the official receiver acts as the trustee in bankruptcy.

This mix of private insolvency practitioners and Insolvency Service officials, along with a handful of bankruptcy judges and registrars, are the people who administer and supervise bankrupt people and their estates. These people are sometimes officious and unpleasant, although there are pockets of courtesy to be found. It is this officious attitude towards bankrupt people which often causes more problems for them than the law itself. Indeed, those of us who run the Bankruptcy Association came to the conclusion long ago that much of bankruptcy law itself is fairly reasonable and innocuous, with some cruel exceptions (the law relating to the seizing of inheritances, for example, can give rise to some obscenely cruel and sad outcomes for the unprepared). It is the way and the manner in which the law is administered, however, that causes much of the pain.

It is a sad fact of life in Britain that those who find themselves in a position of authority often abuse that position, in order to humiliate others. This attitude problem is to be found not only in bankruptcy matters, but in many other areas of life too. If people behaved properly towards each other, most of the unpleasantness which exists in life would be virtually removed.

When and Why to Go Bankrupt

Few people relish the prospect of going bankrupt. They see it as a humiliating process and, indeed, it is. Some have to be dragged through the process kicking and screaming. Others are glad of the relief from pursuing creditors that a bankruptcy order brings. These internalised personal feelings often mean that individual people in debt are their own worst advisers. People in financial trouble should try to set aside their internalised feelings (no easy matter) and look at their problems objectively.

Take the hypothetical case of Peter who has run a business which has failed. He has sold his home in an attempt to stave off business collapse, but in the end he has failed and has no assets left. Peter is now in rented accommodation, unemployed and with tens of thousands of pounds of debts which are causing him desperate worry.

In this example, Peter has, in effect, already suffered most of the worst effects of business failure, ie loss of his home and occupation. He now stands to gain some relief from a bankruptcy, although he may not relish the prospect. He will then be protected from his creditors. During the course of the bankruptcy, as long as he does not inherit or win money, or earn more than he needs to live to a reasonable standard, he will not be required to make any payments to his trustee in bankruptcy. Upon discharge he will be free to rebuild his life anew.

It is this kind of pragmatic reasoning which needs to be applied to people with financial problems. People in debt can be compared to the captain of a sinking ship. A prudent captain will do all he can to save his ship from sinking. It would be foolish if the ship were to go down with all hands, as a result of his efforts. At some point he must decide if the position is hopeless and then save his crew and himself and what possessions he can, by taking to the lifeboats. Bankruptcy may be, in many cases, the lifeboat which a person in debt must take to, after considering the alternatives.

2

Alternatives to Bankruptcy

Most people are keen to avoid bankruptcy, if at all possible. The stigma and other ramifications of bankruptcy are severe enough to make most people think twice before taking this step. There are several formal ways to avoid bankruptcy and there are also informal ways. In the writer's experience most of the formal ways are of little practical use, except in rare circumstances.

The formal legal ways and informal ways to try to avoid bankruptcy in England and Wales are as follows:

Administration Orders

Individuals with debts of less than £5,000, and with at least one judgement debt recorded against them, may apply to their local county court for an administration order to be made at the discretion of the district judge. It will involve an examination of the debtor, usually in private, regarding the debts and income available. The order will usually be granted if unsecured debts total less than £5,000.

The making of an administration order means that all debts notified to the court are brought under a single umbrella, administered by the county court staff. The debtor will be required to make regular payments to the court of an agreed amount. This sum is then divided between the creditors, according to the terms of the order.

The operation of these orders is at the discretion of local district judges. Debt definitions as to the distinction between secured debts and unsecured debts vary, depending upon local operating rules. Furthermore, the district judge has powers to order a sum to be repaid which is less than the total amount owed. Again, local operating rules vary in this respect and it is necessary for enquiries to be made at the appropriate local county court, regarding their precise procedures and rules.

It should be noted that the administration order procedure is only available in England and Wales. It is not available in Scotland and Northern Ireland and, at the time of writing, no similar procedure is in operation in those two countries.

Individual Voluntary Arrangements

The Insolvency Act 1986, which came into effect at the beginning of 1987, opened up another route to avoid bankruptcy.

It is now possible for individual debtors to enter into a formal voluntary arrangement known as an IVA (individual voluntary arrangement). These arrangements are legal contracts for the satisfaction of debts, either in whole or in part, and such arrangements, if voted in, are binding on all unsecured creditors, subject to limited technical exceptions which may cause difficulties.

I was very keen on these arrangements when they first became available and encouraged hundreds of people to take this route. However, bitter experience of watching them fail, time after time, often because of excessive demands made by creditors, has left me wary of recommending this course of action.

A voluntary arrangement is an offer made to unsecured creditors, by an individual in financial trouble, to perhaps dispose of assets and/or make a contribution from future earnings, to pay out a dividend to those unsecured creditors in full settlement of their debts. Secured creditors may also be bound by the arrangement as long as they have been given notice of their entitlement to vote. Their vote only counts, however, if they value their security and it is less than the total amount owed, in which case their vote counts to the extent of the difference. Secured creditors nevertheless remain entitled to enforce their security, unless they have agreed not to do so. This means, for example, that they can repossess a house if the mortgage is in arrears. They cannot, however, then pursue the individual for any shortfall arising after the sale, but must claim for it within the arrangement. If, by the time they do enforce their security, the arrangement has ended and they have not claimed in it for the anticipated shortfall, they are still bound by the fact that it was approved.

A proposal must be made to and through an insolvency practitioner, who is a person specifically authorised to deal with such matters. Insolvency practitioners are usually qualified as either accountants or solicitors. In practice, they help prepare the proposal and should act as an independent intermediary between the debtor and the creditors, thereby ensuring that the proposal is realistic and represents a fair balance between the interests of all concerned. Once a proposal has been prepared, an application is made to the court for an interim order. This protects the debtor from further legal action by creditors. That protection prevents the issue of a bankruptcy petition or the hearing of a petition which has already been issued. The purpose is to maintain the current position until the creditors have had the opportunity to consider the proposal, at a meeting called by the insolvency practitioner for that purpose. Such a meeting will be called, unless the insolvency practitioner reports to the court that there is no reasonable prospect of creditors agreeing.

Arrangements may involve the disposal of assets, so that the proceeds may be shared amongst the creditors. Payments may be made by the debtor from future income or from trading receipts. Sometimes funds may be made available by a friend or relative, in return for creditors accepting the proposal. Any combination is possible. Often the debtor will wish to keep his home, in return for payments from his future earnings or from a third party.

All creditors may vote on the proposal, either by being present in person, by sending a representative or by sending a postal vote. The votes of secured creditors only count to the extent that their security is insufficient to cover their lending. Voting power is according to money owed to individual creditors. It then requires the agreement of 75 per cent, by money value, of those creditors who trouble to vote, and whose votes are valid, to turn the proposal into a binding voluntary arrangement. This is subject to the proviso that there are at least 50 per cent in favour, ignoring the votes of connected persons, ie 'close relatives.'

If a voluntary arrangement succeeds, then bankruptcy is avoided. In law, individuals may then incur further credit. In reality, their credit rating is ruined because voluntary arrangements are recorded by credit reference agencies.

The costs of setting up the voluntary arrangement and supervising the implementation of it, if approved, should come from the monies which the arrangement provides to be distributed to creditors. In reality, however, most insolvency practitioners will be unwilling to act unless some, if not all, of the initial costs are paid to them in advance. This is because, if the arrangement is not approved, there will be no funds to cover their fees. Depending on the complexity of the case and the area in which the debtor resides, these costs can range between £1,000 and £5,000.

Anyone entering into a voluntary arrangement must adhere strictly to the agreed terms, otherwise the insolvency practitioner supervising the arrangement has little choice but to apply for the bankruptcy of the person involved. A good arrangement should allow some flexibility in the event of unforeseen circumstances. When arrangements do fail mid-term, the misery of the debt problem has simply been extended and because there are bankruptcy costs as well as the costs of the arrangement which went before, creditors also suffer a detriment.

It should also be pointed out that even if a bankruptcy order has been made against an individual, then a voluntary arrangement may still be attempted. If successful, it will have the effect of lifting the bankruptcy order.

There are many sharks in the insolvency world, some advertise in national newspapers, claiming to be able to save people from bankruptcy. These sharks often simply refer people to insolvency practitioners, collecting a fat fee for themselves, en route. From their own selfish point of view, it is in the interests of these sharks to encourage people to go for voluntary arrangements, when this may not be the best option for the debtor. Those who are in financial difficulty should make sure they contact someone appropriately experienced to give them guidance, such as the Bankruptcy Association.

To sum up, individual voluntary arrangements should be approached with extreme caution and they should only be considered if there is some real, practical benefit to the person involved. The mere avoidance of bankruptcy itself is not, in my view, sufficient justification, although there are others who think it is.

This procedure is available to people resident in Northern Ireland as well as England and Wales, but is not available in Scotland.

Deeds of Arrangement

These were the predecessors to the more modern voluntary arrangements and for some curious reason were carried forward from old bankruptcy law into the Insolvency Act 1986. Only a handful are registered each year and they are, for all practical purposes, extinct. Anyone curious about these rarely used procedures should refer to a more detailed bankruptcy textbook.

Informal Arrangements

In addition to these formal procedures to avoid bankruptcy, it is possible to try informal methods.

The simplest, least expensive and, in my wide experience, most effective way of coming to an arrangement with creditors is by direct negotiation. Debtors with good communication skills may attempt to reach agreement with creditors whereby they repay a percentage of their debts in full settlement. Solicitors, accountants, CABs and other money advice agencies will sometimes carry out these negotiations for debtors, with varying degrees of skill and success. A major problem facing many debtors is the inadequacy and incompetence of solicitors, accountants and other advisers.

I founded the Bankruptcy Association initially as a specialist agency to provide competent and effective advice. We now carry out hundreds of negotiations with creditors each year, reaching agreements to avoid the necessity of bankruptcy. Many agreements have been reached with creditors whereby they have accepted a few pence in the pound, in full settlement of particular debts. There are technical difficulties in ensuring that informal arrangements are legally binding. These can, however, be overcome if the matter is approached in the proper manner.

Of course, it is not always possible to negotiate a settlement, sometimes a single creditor owed a relatively small amount may refuse an agreement made with the main creditors. Nonetheless successful conclusions are reached in a large percentage of the cases we handle.

It is possible to set up these informal arrangements in every country of the United Kingdom.

3

Going Bankrupt

The previous chapter describes the methods of avoiding bankruptcy. In many cases, however, it simply cannot be avoided, either because creditors are determined to bankrupt those who owe them money, or because debtors have found it impossible to reach agreement with creditors. In such instances bankruptcy will ensue.

There are three ways to go bankrupt. A creditor owed at least £750 can bring a petition against a person owing them that money, or a debtor can bring a petition against himself. A person involved in an individual voluntary arrangement can also be bankrupted by the supervisor of his arrangement, if he fails to comply with the terms of the arrangement. There are no restrictions on who can bankrupt themselves in England, Wales and Northern Ireland, although there are restrictions in Scotland (see chapter 8).

Creditor's Petition

A creditor may bring a bankruptcy petition against anyone who owes him £750 or more (as at 21 July 1995), or two or more creditors may combine together, as long as the debts equal that amount. The normal procedure is that a creditor must first serve a statutory demand on the debtor, demanding payment of the debt within three weeks. If the debt is not paid within this time,

11

then the creditor can proceed to issue a bankruptcy petition against the debtor. If someone disputes the debt claimed in the statutory demand, then an application may be made to have it set aside.

If, however, a creditor has a judgement against a debtor, has issued execution and has a return from the bailiff to the effect that there are insufficient goods which can be seized to cover the amount owed, then that creditor can present a bankruptcy petition, without first serving a statutory demand.

The debtor must then pay the debt and the associated costs before the date of the bankruptcy hearing, otherwise a bankruptcy order will be made. Even if the particular debt and costs are paid, the court may still make a bankruptcy order if another creditor then moves in and takes over the action.

It is sometimes possible, at the discretion of the court, to have a hearing for bankruptcy adjourned. The usual grounds for such an adjournment are that within a short time the debtor can raise the money to clear his debts. The court will need to be convinced that this is likely to happen fairly soon. It is worth mentioning a little known, and even less tested, section of the Insolvency Act, section 271 subsection (3). This subsection provides that a court 'may' dismiss a bankruptcy petition if the debtor has made an offer to give reasonable security in respect of the debt or to satisfy it in a reasonable way, not necessarily involving full payment of the debt, and the creditor has unreasonably refused the offer. This is of particular relevance when dealing with a vindictive creditor who wants to see a person bankrupt, regardless of the consequences for himself, the debtor or other creditors.

If a debtor intends to submit to a bankruptcy petition, it is unnecessary for him to attend the court in person, but it would be appropriate to write to the court, apologising for his absence.

Debtor's Petition

A debtor can bring his own bankruptcy petition by obtaining a bankruptcy petition form from his local county court (or from the High Court in the Strand for those living within the London insolvency district). On completion of this form, which lists debts, assets and other information, a telephone call to the court should be made, to arrange an appointment for a bankruptcy hearing. The completed form is then taken to the court with the necessary fee in cash (this is £270 for an individual and £500 for a partnership, as at 21 July 1995). The current fee should be ascertained with the relevant court. A bankruptcy order will normally be made immediately, on the presentation of the fee and the petition. If it is vital that a bankruptcy order be made immediately and the local court for some reason is not available (some courts do not have a district judge available every weekday), then an order may be sought from an alternative court. Each local court should know which is the alternative court to be used.

In cases, however, where a debtor declares assets of at least £2,000 and debts of less than £20,000, then the court may not make a bankruptcy order, but may send the debtor to see an insolvency practitioner to ascertain if a voluntary arrangement would be an appropriate option. (It is quite beyond the writer's understanding as to why this odd provision is part of our bankruptcy laws). Voluntary arrangements are explained in the previous chapter.

The Immediate Aftermath of a Bankruptcy Order

Once a bankruptcy order has been made, then all the assets and property of the bankrupt person (with certain exceptions explained later) vest in the trustee in bankruptcy, who initially is the official receiver, an employee of the Insolvency Service (an executive agency of the Department of Trade and Industry). There are around forty official receivers' offices in England and Wales, each with its own official receiver and supporting staff of examiners and others.

If a debtor has brought a bankruptcy petition against himself, then he usually speaks by telephone to his local official receiver from the court, after the bankruptcy order has been made. The official receiver will ask for details of the bankrupt's bank accounts and other information. He will normally arrange an appointment for the bankrupt to attend his office for an interview. Depending on the information given by the bankrupt to the official receiver, then he might arrange for agents to immediately visit the bankrupt's business address to seize assets. It is very unusual, however,

13

for the official receiver to send anyone to the bankrupt's home address in England, Wales and Northern Ireland. In Scotland the reverse is true and Scottish readers are referred to chapter 8.

Any bank or building society accounts in which the bankrupt has an interest (including any joint accounts) will normally be frozen immediately by the official receiver. Thus a husband and wife with a joint account would have any funds in the account frozen, even if only one of them go bankrupt. The money belonging to the non-bankrupt spouse would be returned in due course, but this will take time and could cause great inconvenience and distress. For this and other reasons, it is important that the non-bankrupt spouse open their own separate account before the bankruptcy, in order to avoid these problems.

If a creditor has brought the petition, then the bankrupt will usually be contacted immediately by the official receiver either by telephone or letter. Again, if the official receiver has reason to believe that there are substantial assets in place on business premises, then he may send someone immediately to seize these goods.

This is a brief outline of events which take place immediately after the making of the bankruptcy order. The sequence of these events vary from area to area. In some areas the official receiver's office is close to the court and a debtor bringing his own petition might be sent around immediately to the official receiver's office. The main point to be understood is that very rapid moves are made to seize the assets and property of the bankrupt. Readers need to be aware of this fact.

Exempt Property

Certain property is exempt from bankruptcy proceedings and it is worth quoting the precise letter of the law because, over the years, I have come across many instances whereby official receivers and trustees have overstepped the law and seized exempt property. The appropriate legal reference is section 283 of the Insolvency Act 1986. This section states that all property of the bankrupt vests in the trustee except for:

'such tools, books, vehicles and other items of equipment as are necessary to the bankrupt for use personally by him in his employment, business or vocation.' (section 283 subsection 2(a))'

'such clothing, bedding, furniture, household equipment and provisions as are necessary for satisfying the basic domestic needs of the bankrupt and his family.' (section 283 subsection 2(b))'

The rule of thumb applied by the authorities is that they will allow a bankrupt to keep any particular item referred to above which is worth less than £500. Therefore a car worth more than £500 would be seized, as would a piece of antique furniture worth thousands of pounds. An ordinary person living in a typical semi-detached home with household equipment of normal value would be left with everything intact. Likewise a builder or photographer, or any one else running a business, should be left with all items of equipment and vehicles worth less than £500 each. It should be emphasised that sometimes agents of the official receiver use intimidating tactics and the bankrupt's ignorance of the law to overstep these rules and seize exempt items of property. No reader of this book should be so intimidated and strong objections should be made if anyone tries to overstep this mark.

If a vehicle worth more than £500 which is necessary for a bankrupt's business or employment is seized by the official receiver or trustee, then the cost of a reasonable replacement must be allowed – if there are sufficient monies available in the estate after the expenses have been taken (an unlikely scenario in many bankruptcies).

The Interview

Every bankrupt person must attend their local official receiver's office for a personal interview. This typically lasts for 2 to 3 hours and is carried out by an examiner, a member of the official receiver's staff. The interview may be much longer if it is a complex case. The main purpose is to examine the causes of the bankruptcy and to check that no wrongdoing or fraudulent activity is involved.

Statement of Affairs

Before the interview takes place, the bankrupt is usually sent a complex form to complete. This is known as the statement of affairs and the bankrupt is required to complete this form which examines in detail his financial history and other matters. This is usually checked by the examiner, at the interview, to ensure that it is completely accurate. Again, the object is to ascertain that no fraud has taken place and that all the bankrupt's assets have been disclosed. There is no need to employ anyone to help complete this form. If the bankrupt has difficulties with the form he should contact the official receiver's office and ask for their advice.

Meeting of Creditors Following Bankruptcy Order

Once a bankruptcy order has been made, the official receiver has twelve weeks from that date to decide whether or not to summon a meeting of creditors. The official receiver must also call such a meeting if it is requested by sufficient creditors. A meeting is also called if the official receiver thinks there are sufficient assets to merit the appointment of an insolvency practitioner to deal with the estate. A bankrupt must attend this meeting if requested, but in my experience, it is extremely unusual for a bankrupt to be asked to attend.

Public Examination

The official receiver may apply to the court for the public examination of the bankrupt, at any time before discharge from bankruptcy. The bankrupt must attend such an examination, if the official receiver requests it. If creditors to the value of not less than half the debts of the bankrupt request a public examination, then this must also take place, if the court agrees to the request. Public examinations are very rare events and they usually only take place for more spectacular bankruptcies, where there is a strong suspicion of fraud or other wrongdoing. If a public examination does take place, then the bankrupt must answer questions under oath, put to him by the official receiver and the court.

It should be pointed out that an insolvency practitioner or the official receiver has extensive powers to to ask for information about the bankrupt from anyone who may have information about the bankrupt's financial affairs. Information can be sort informally or by summoning the relevant person before the court to be examined under oath.

Private Examinations

Bankrupts can also be called in for private examination about their financial affairs by official receivers and trustees throughout the period of their bankruptcy. They can also be examined in court. These examinations nearly always occur when the trustee or official receiver believes a bankrupt has hidden away assets and/or property, or has improperly disposed of them.

Bankruptcy in Death

There is a famous saying that the only two certainties in life are death and taxation. In reality, the former does not enable a debtor to escape the pursuit of his assets by creditors. A court may make an insolvency administration order (this is a bankruptcy order by another name) against a deceased debtor's estate. A creditor or the debtor's personal representative may also apply for such an order. The estate is then dealt with in the usual way. The court, however, may make special orders as to how matters are to be dealt with. If a bankruptcy order is made against someone, and that person subsequently dies shortly afterwards, then the estate is still dealt with under bankruptcy rules – and not under an insolvency administration order.

4

Restrictions and Problems of Being a Bankrupt

For anyone in debt, bankruptcy brings one huge overwhelming benefit. It frees the bankrupt from pursuit by his creditors for debts which he owes. In due course he is released from these debts. It should be noted that a bankrupt is not freed from court fines, maintenance, or child support agency orders, nor from any debts which may have arisen as a result of fraud. Aside from these exceptions, it brings a substantial relief to the debtor.

In return for this single benefit the bankrupt has to live with a whole series of restrictions and difficulties throughout the period of the bankruptcy and often beyond it. The main problems are as follows:

Bank Accounts

Any bank accounts held by the bankrupt are normally frozen immediately and, in most cases, subsequently closed, as few financial institutions are willing to give normal banking facilities to a bankrupt. For example, a bankrupt person will find it virtually impossible to obtain a cheque guarantee card. In addition, strictly speaking, a bankrupt may not operate a bank account without the permission of his trustee (this does not apply to building society

18

accounts). This double block eliminates normal banking facilities for most bankrupts.

Building Society Accounts

Most bankrupts find it easy to open a variety of building society savings accounts. Many of these provide a card for making withdrawals from cash points and allow the setting up of standing orders. They also provide a means of receiving wage payments, but they do not provide a cheque book or a cheque card. A bankrupt must never accrue savings in his own name, as these are liable to be seized by the trustee in bankruptcy.

Obtaining Future Credit

It is an offence for a bankrupt to obtain credit of more than £250 from any future creditor, without disclosing that he is bankrupt. If a creditor is aware of the bankruptcy and offers credit of more than £250 then this is acceptable, although the bankrupt would be wise to obtain the creditor's consent in writing to avoid possible repercussions.

Gas, Electricity, Water and Telephone Supplies

Gas, electricity, water and telephone bills do not have to be paid up to the date of the bankruptcy order as these fall into the bankruptcy. These suppliers can, and sometimes do, cut off supplies unless a deposit is paid or other arrangements are made about the payment of future accounts.

Council Tax

This is a daily tax, therefore any council tax due up to the date of the bankruptcy goes into the bankruptcy. Sums due to the council from the date of the bankruptcy order, however, must be paid. In the case of a husband and wife living together if the husband goes bankrupt, then the wife would be responsible for the council tax.

Property

Most people think of property as referring to bricks and mortar. The term 'property' for the purposes of bankruptcy law has a much wider meaning. Correspondence from trustees and official receivers may use this word applying to a wide variety of items, such as royalty contracts, pensions, life policies, houses, or anything else which may have a money value.

Control of Assets by Trustee

If a bankrupt has assets, then an insolvency practitioner will be appointed to take over from the official receiver. He will dispose of major assets, such as the bankrupt's home. If the bankrupt has no assets to cover the fees of these private trustees, then the official receiver will act as trustee in such cases.

Whether the trustee in bankruptcy is an official receiver or a private insolvency practitioner, the bankrupt is under a legal obligation to co-operate with him, particularly regarding providing information about his assets and property. The bankrupt is also under a legal obligation to inform the trustee of any change in his financial circumstances until he is discharged from the bankruptcy, eg if he receives a salary increase.

Excess Value Vests in Trustee

Where a trustee believes that the value of certain items which are exempted under section 283 of the Insolvency Act (explained in the previous chapter) exceed the cost of a reasonable replacement, then he can claim these items for the benefit of the creditors. If, however, there are funds available in the bankrupt's estate, then the trustee must provide funds to the bankrupt for a reasonable replacement of any such items. The rule of thumb generally being applied is that any item or piece of equipment worth more than £500 would normally be attacked in this way. This is a grey area of the law and has to be negotiated on a case by case basis.

Disclaimer

A trustee in bankruptcy has the power to disclaim any onerous property or unprofitable contracts. This enables the trustee to wash his hands of any problems which may arise in dealing with the bankrupt's property. He could, for example, disclaim responsibility for a dangerous building. Anyone suffering a loss as a result of a disclaimer by a trustee can claim in the bankruptcy, to the extent of that loss.

Running a Business

If a bankrupt is in business, then he will lose control of all his principle assets, as these will be sold. In many cases this will mean the business will have to close. If someone was running a shop for example, then all the stock in the shop would be seized and disposed of. This will effectively bring an end to the business.

There is nothing in law, however, to prevent a bankrupt from continuing to run a business and some do. Many bankrupt plumbers, builders, accountants and book-keepers, for example, simply continue to trade, as do many others. A bankrupt must trade in the name under which he was made bankrupt, and he must remember the restrictions about obtaining credit. If a bankrupt does continue to trade, he needs to reach agreement with the trustee in bankruptcy as to how any profits will be divided. A trustee in bankruptcy may also, in certain cases, continue to run a bankrupt's business if this will benefit creditors (by selling off the remaining stocks of a business, for example). The trustee may employ the bankrupt to do this for him, or he can appoint a special manager.

Redirection of Mail

The official receiver or the trustee may apply to the court to have a bankrupt's mail redirected. This action is usually taken in cases where it is felt that the bankrupt has not been truthful about his affairs. Once examined, it is then forwarded to the bankrupt. A prominent legal academic, however, believes that this provision would not stand up to examination in the European courts, if it was ever brought to them for examination. He believes such mail is the property of the sender and not the property of the bankrupt, the intended recipient.

Life Assurance

The trustees will dispose of any life assurance policies owned by the bankrupt which have acquired a surrender value. The non-bankrupt spouse will be given the opportunity to buy any joint policies for half of the surrender value of the policy. The non-bankrupt wife of a bankrupt may take out an insurance policy on the life of her husband, making sure that she is the direct beneficiary in the event of his death. If a husband and wife are both bankrupt they cannot cross insure like this, as the trustee would seize any benefits. In such circumstances, the best they can do is to ensure any life policies are set up in trust, with their children being the beneficiaries. Great care and thought should be taken over these matters.

Pensions

The position with pensions is a complete and utter minefield! In recent correspondence with the Inspector General of Bankruptcy I was told that the Insolvency Service take the view that pensions are a 'thing in action' and therefore form part of the property of the bankrupt, rendering them open to attack by trustees in bankruptcy. Christopher Garwood, a specialist lawyer from Carrick Read Insolvency, stated in his review notes on the original script of this book that there is no doubt in his mind that both the lump sum element and income of pensions can be attacked by a trustee.

At the time of writing, no clear legal precedent on the matter has been established. As a result, the position regarding pensions is very confused and confusing, although the tide generally seems to be running against bankrupts. Some pension companies are giving in to the demands of trustees, others are not. Some trustees themselves make no effort to attack pensions, others act aggressively.

The only practical advice I can currently offer to any bankrupt is that he should resist, by all the means at his disposable, any attempt to attack either his pension income or lump sum, but should not expect to win. Complaints should be made by bankrupts to the pension trustees and administrators and to Members of Parliament, where pensions are threatened. Legal action may also be taken if it can be funded, after taking appropriate advice.

Contracts and Leases

In general terms, bankruptcy terminates any contracts or leases to which a bankrupt is a party. Where a loss has been suffered by a creditor or a bankrupt as a result of a contract between them, an application can be made to the court by either party for an order for damages. Any damages which the bankrupt was ordered to pay would then simply rank as another bankruptcy debt. Any payment received by a bankrupt would vest in his trustee.

Where someone who is bankrupt is party to a joint contract or lease with another person who is not bankrupt, then the person who is not bankrupt can sue, and be sued, in respect of that contract, without reference to the bankrupt person.

After Acquired Property

Any property acquired by the bankrupt before discharge can be taken by the trustee in bankruptcy. Thus a bankrupt who won the national lottery could have the proceeds seized from him. The bankrupt is only allowed to keep income necessary for reasonable living expenses and certain exempted items, as explained in the previous chapter. Any savings accrued by a bankrupt may be seized. In other words, a bankrupt is expected to live in a very modest way, until he is discharged.

After being declared bankrupt, any legacies or inheritances of that bankrupt becomes the property of the trustee. It is very important, therefore, that relatives are made aware of this, so that they may make the necessary amendments to their wills. People often neglect to do this, hoping that ageing parents and other relatives will not die during the bankruptcy period. Some of the most distressing calls I receive are from bankrupts who get caught short in this way. This is a very important matter to which all bankrupts should immediately attend.

The Matrimonial Home

All property of the bankrupt (except exempt items listed in the previous chapter) may be sold by the trustee in bankruptcy, including the home of the bankrupt, whether he owns it entirely or in part. The non bankrupt spouse of a bankrupt is normally entitled to a half share of the value of the home, whether or not the house is in joint names (this does not apply in Scotland). In addition, there is a twelve month protection from the trustee in bankruptcy before he can force the sale of the home if the bankrupt's wife and/or children, or someone else, also reside there. The non-bankrupt spouse is given the opportunity to save the home by purchasing the beneficial interest of the bankrupt. The trustee will require the value of the bankrupt's share, although he may make an allowance for the fact that he does not have to pay the costs of a sale in such cases. Thus the non-bankrupt spouse may have to raise slightly less than half of the equity in the property, to secure the home.

If there is no equity in the home, or negative equity, then the non-bankrupt spouse may purchase the bankrupt's interest, usually for a nominal amount of between £1 and £100, plus the legal fees incurred in the transfer. In such cases, if there is a joint mortgage, this can remain in place, although the beneficial interest of the bankrupt spouse has been sold to the non-bankrupt one. This means there is no requirement to raise a new mortgage. The Bankruptcy Association arranges scores of such transactions each year.

If the non-bankrupt spouse does not wish, or is unable, to save the home in this way, then after 12 months the trustee may apply for possession and sale of the property, if he so chooses. He will only do this, of course, if there is equity in the property. If there is negative equity, the bankrupt may continue to live in the property, as long as he services the mortgage. The trustee must obtain a court order for possession of the property, or the agreement of the occupants, before he may sell the home. This provides further time to negotiate with him.

In cases where both husband and wife are bankrupt then one cannot buy the other's share. In such cases the home will be lost. If a husband and wife who are both bankrupt live in a house with negative equity, then they may also stay there as long as they service the mortgage. If there is still no equity in the home when they receive their discharges (see chapter 6), then they may repurchase their interest in the home from the trustee in bankruptcy. A trustee can sometimes be persuaded to wait until this happens. Alternatively, a third party, perhaps a family member, may purchase the house.

Some bankrupts who have homes with negative equity at the date of their bankruptcy are left with the impression, because of casual remarks from staff at official receivers' offices, that they will not be troubled about it. A bankrupt's interest in a property automatically vests in the trustee for ever, unless it is legally purchased from him. If this transaction is not carried out, then a trustee in bankruptcy can appear on the horizon, even years after discharge, and sell the home because equity has subsequently arisen in the property. It is important, therefore, that bankrupts understand the position.

A final important point on this matter is that bankrupt people and their families should try to sort out the position regarding the family home as soon as possible after bankruptcy has occurred.

Charge on the Home

In cases where there is very little equity in a bankrupt's home, or where there is negative equity, then the trustee sometimes places a charge on the property to stake his claim to the bankrupt's share of the property, should it increase in value in the future. The trustee places this charge so that he can close down the initial administration of the bankruptcy. Even if the trustee does not place a charge on a bankrupt's property, he is entitled to claim the bankrupt's share of any future equity which may arise, unless arrangements are made as described in the preceding section on the matrimonial home.

Income Payments Orders

A bankrupt is allowed to keep that element of his income necessary to meet all necessary living expenses and travel expenses, in connection with his employment or business. A proportion of any surplus income must be paid to the trustee in bankruptcy. At the interview following the making of the bankruptcy order, a bankrupt has to draw up a budget detailing these expenses. The amount which a bankrupt may be called upon to pay will depend on the results of this budget exercise. If a bankrupt has a spouse or partner who is working, then it may be assumed that this other person is responsible for half of the budget. Bankrupts should remember to include at least the following items in their household budget, as appropriate:

Mortgage or rent
Council tax
Water rates
Electricity
Gas
Other fuel
TV licence
Telephone
Prescriptions
Car tax and insurance
Car Maintenance
Bus fares
Taxi fares
Newspapers
Home repairs/maintenance
Clothes, shoes etc
Food
Sundries

Often a voluntary payment is agreed. In cases where there is a dispute over the amount to be paid, then the trustee may apply to the court for an income payments order to be made. The court will decide on the amount to be paid and the length of period of the order (up to a maximum of three years). Once an income payments order is made, then this binds the bankrupt to pay the amount decided by the court at pain of being sent to prison, in the event of default. If a bankrupt's financial circumstances change for the worse, he may apply to the court to have the order varied, so that he pays a lower amount. If his financial circumstances improve, then the trustee may apply to the court to vary the order, to increase the amount being paid.

In practice, this whole business of making payments is often a very hit and miss procedure, based on arbitrary attitudes of different official receivers and trustees. In the practical aspects of bankruptcy administration, there are tremendous variations in the treatment of people.

Income Tax Refunds

If a bankrupt receives a tax refund after the bankruptcy, connected with money earned before the bankruptcy, then the trustee is entitled to reclaim this from the bankrupt.

Income Tax Advantage

One of the few advantages of bankruptcy is that if a bankrupt remains in the same employment as he was in before bankruptcy, then he sometimes pays no tax in the tax year in which he was bankrupted (this does not apply to self-employed people). Current tax rules, however, are complex and fluid and this advantage may not always apply. Bankrupts should, however, be aware that there may possibly be a tax advantage.

Redundancy Payments

Any redundancy money received during the course of the bankruptcy may be claimed by the trustee in bankruptcy. With the co-operation of the employer, however, it may be possible to structure severance pay in such a way that it is treated as income and therefore not as easily attackable by the trustee.

Debts Arising After Bankruptcy

If a bankrupt's home is repossessed or sold after the date of the bankruptcy, and there is a shortfall on the mortgage, then this is known as a contingent debt and forms part of the bankruptcy. Although the debt arises, in a sense after bankruptcy, it is really only quantified then. Some building societies do not understand this and try to sue bankrupts for the shortfalls, treating the debts as if they had arisen after the date of the bankruptcy. This is an error on their part and a bankrupt should send any such claims to the official receiver, so that he may deal with them.

In the event of other debts which really do arise after the bankruptcy, then the bankrupt is liable for these. Any credit or contract entered into after the date of the bankruptcy is the liability of the bankrupt. It is therefore possible to be bankrupted again, even whilst bankrupt, for debts which arise after the date of the original bankruptcy. A second bankruptcy is a serious business and is dealt with in chapter 6.

Creditors Cannot Stand Outside Bankruptcy

Certain debts still have to be paid, even in bankruptcy. For example, a speeding fine would have to be paid. Maintenance payments and child support orders also have to be honoured, as do any debts arising as a result of fraud.

All other categories of debt form part of the bankruptcy and the bankrupt is safe from pursuit from these creditors. I have come across, however, many instances where creditors have mistakenly tried to pursue bankrupts unlawfully for debts.

Debts to Spouse

Where a bankrupt has borrowed money from a spouse, then the spouse is the last in line creditor. The spouse will only have that debt repaid by the trustee if all the other creditors and the costs of the bankruptcy can be paid first, an unusual circumstance. Thus, the spouse of a bankrupt is unlikely to recoup any money loaned to a bankrupt.

If the spouse, however, has a security for money loaned to a partner then they will receive precedence, eg when a charge has been taken on the family home for money loaned. It should be pointed out that any spouse lending their partner money would be wise to legally secure such lending, to avoid being a last in line creditor.

Limited Companies

A bankrupt cannot take part either directly or indirectly in promoting, forming or managing a limited company of any sort, unless he obtains the permission of the court. It is possible to work for a limited company, for example, as a sales manager. The key point is that if a bankrupt is involved in a limited company he must make it clear to any creditors of the company that he is not involved in the financial side of the company. If a bankrupt involved with a limited company gives the impression to creditors that he is managing the company, and the company folds, he could be in serious trouble.

Exclusion from Certain Offices and Jobs

A bankrupt is excluded from certain public offices. He cannot be a member of parliament, a local councillor or a school governor, for example.

Solicitors, accountants and chartered surveyors will face serious professional bars. A bankrupt solicitor will probably not be allowed to have a private practice but he may work for others, for example, for a local authority. A bankrupt accountant will have his professional status withdrawn, but he may still prepare accounts for sole traders. There are hundreds of bankrupt accountants, busy at their trade, as I write.

Bankrupts cannot engage in selling financial products, so they are effectively barred from the financial services industry. There may be problems with certain other jobs if the job specifications exclude bankrupts.

Most jobs, however, are not affected. Many teachers, for example, go bankrupt each year and it rarely has any effect upon their careers.

Disposal of Assets at an Undervalue

It is illegal for a bankrupt to dispose of assets at an undervalue. If such a transaction is discovered, these assets may be reclaimed by the trustee. In addition, the bankrupt may be charged with committing an offence. The most common scenario is where a husband signs over the family home to his wife, without payment, before a bankruptcy occurs. This transaction will not stand up if it occurred within five years of the date of the bankruptcy, if the husband was insolvent at the time, or became insolvent as a result of making the gift. There is a dual definition of insolvency. It means either that the bankrupt could not meet his debts as and when due, or that his assets were not equal to his debts, as a result of the transaction. The burden of evidence is on the bankrupt to prove that he was solvent at the time.

Even if the husband was solvent at the time of gifting the property, and did not become insolvent as a result of making the gift, then it must have occurred at least two years before the date of the bankruptcy, for the transaction to stand up.

The point should also be made that if there is a transfer of assets of any sort between husband and wife, they should have it properly recorded, to show that it was on the basis of a 'sale,' and not a 'gift.'

The same rules apply to any other assets or money.

Assets Abroad

A bankrupt is obliged to disclose any assets which he owns world-wide. Many people have property in Spain or France these days. This property may be seized and sold by the trustee. If a bankrupt has debts or claims against his property in other countries, then foreign courts may not grant a UK trustee the right to seize those assets.

Civil Actions in Progress at Time of Bankruptcy

Any civil legal actions being pursued against the bankrupt, other than matrimonial proceedings, die at the date of the bankruptcy. In the same way, civil actions being pursued by the bankrupt against others vest in the trustee in bankruptcy, except actions arising over personal injury. Thus it falls to the trustee to pursue any legal actions of the bankrupt. He will rarely do so because, in effect, he is gambling with creditors' money to pursue such cases and he would be liable to the creditors if he lost. He would not, therefore, pursue any action unless his costs were underwritten by creditors, an unlikely scenario. A new law, however, has now made it possible to agree conditional fee arrangements with solicitors on a no win/no fee basis. This may, over time, mean that trustees carry forward more actions than previously, on this basis. The trustee may also, and currently often does, pass a right of action back to the bankrupt. Unless, however, there is an agreement between the bankrupt and the trustee saying otherwise, then the trustee would receive all monies awarded to the bankrupt. It is common practice, however, to reach agreement with the trustee to split any legal awards on a fifty fifty basis, so that the bankrupt has an incentive to pursue a case.

A bankrupt may, however, sue for personal injury, due to a car accident, for example, although he must inform the trustee of the action. The bankrupt may keep for himself any money awarded for pain and suffering. Any money awarded for loss of past earnings would fall to the trustee in bankruptcy. Money awarded for loss of future earnings is a grey legal area and would have to be negotiated. This has applied in the many cases in which I have been involved. Christopher Garwood, the specialist lawyer checking this script, has pointed out that there may be a theoretical claim against such awards, on the basis of them being classed as after acquired property. His advice is that a bankrupt should try to delay, if possible, the settlement of any such claim until discharge from bankruptcy has occurred.

Release of Trustee

When a trustee in bankruptcy has disposed of all of the property and assets of a bankrupt, then the administration of the bankruptcy estate may become dormant. The trustee may then apply to be released from the chore of the paperwork relating to the administration of a 'live case.' This application for release simply frees the trustee from administering the estate. On release, he provides the bankrupt with a statement detailing how the money collected has been dispensed (usually, it has all gone on his fees). Bankrupts sometimes confuse this application for release by the trustee, with their own discharge from bankruptcy. They think that they, too, have been released from their bankruptcy. This is not so. Discharge from bankruptcy is dealt with in chapter 6. The application for the release of the trustee is simply a routine administrative procedure. In simple bankruptcy cases, the trustee may apply for his release a year into the bankruptcy. In more complex cases the trustee might not apply for release until years after the bankrupt has been discharged. This is because the seizure and disposal of a bankrupt's property may take many years, such as where a house takes time to sell.

Bankruptcy Offences

A bankrupt can commit a large number of offences. In the most serious cases, sentences can be as severe as seven years imprisonment, although such severe sentences are very rare. The most common offences that bankrupts commit are the following:

Failing to disclose property
Failing to deliver property or concealing property
Failing to account for loss of property
Failing to deliver required papers and records
Concealing or destroying books or papers
Making material omission in statement of affairs
Making false statements
Fraudulently disposing of property
Obtaining credit without disclosing the bankruptcy
Increasing extent of insolvency through gambling

Bankrupts Living and Working Abroad

The Bankruptcy Association has a worldwide dimension to its work, in that some of its members live and work abroad. Sometimes these members raise mind boggling legal queries with me. There are often no clear answers to their questions because there are so many 'ifs and buts' involved. Cross border insolvency procedures are often extremely complex to unravel, and the international rules are changing day by day. I can, however, offer some general advice on a wide variety of issues which members regularly raise.

First, there is no reason why someone, bankrupt in the UK, cannot live and work abroad. Passports are not confiscated, other than in very rare cases. This could happen where it is feared by the authorities that a bankrupt is trying to escape abroad with money. A bankrupt should, however, inform his official receiver or trustee about his earnings abroad, to comply with his duty to cooperate during the bankruptcy.

Secondly, bankruptcy is jurisdictional. This means that someone bankrupted under UK law is only a bankrupt in the United Kingdom. If that bankrupt moves to Eire, the USA, France or some other foreign country, he is not a bankrupt in that country. He can obtain credit in other countries, as long as he complies with the law in those countries. If, however, he acquires property or assets whilst abroad, and whilst still bankrupt, the trustee in the UK may well be able to seize those assets, if he learns of them.

Thirdly, if someone lives abroad, with debts in the UK he wishes to go bankrupt for, then he must return to England and bankrupt himself in person at the High Court in The Strand, London. He cannot bankrupt himself in his absence, or by post.

Fourthly, someone living abroad can be bankrupted in his absence by creditors in the UK. He would probably not be discharged from his bankruptcy, unless he ensured that he fully cooperated with the trustee and official receiver in providing them with details of his property and affairs, to the best of his ability.

Fifthly, UK bankrupts can be directors of foreign companies, although those companies must not have their main base of operation in the UK. In other words, a UK bankrupt cannot set up a foreign company and operate that company in the UK. He can however, be a director of a French company which operates its business in France. Bankrupts should also check carefully on the internal company laws of foreign countries.

Sixthly, cross border insolvency actions are not uncommon. They can be complex as I indicated above, but they do occur on a regular basis. I know of one case where a woman, whilst living in Sweden, borrowed money from a Swedish bank. She subsequently returned to England without repaying the debt. The Swedish bank eventually tracked her down, obtained judgement against her for the debt in a UK court, and she was then forced to bankrupt herself in the UK. She would probably have been wiser to have bankrupted herself under Swedish law and she could then have returned to the UK, where she would not be a bankrupt.

5

Partnership Bankruptcies

This chapter deals with partnership law as it effects the more typical partnerships comprising for example, of three brothers, a husband and wife team or three or four colleagues. The law for larger partnerships and/or those containing a corporate partner is more complex and is not covered here.

There is a common misconception that if there are three partners in a business partnership which owes £30,000, then each partner is liable for, and can only be pursued for, £10,000. This is not so. Each partner is liable for the entire partnership debt.

Creditors can pursue the entire partnership by having it wound up as a limited company and having the assets of the partnership sold. To complicate matters even further, they can then, at the same time, or later, pursue any or all of the partners into personal bankruptcy, in order to force the sale of their personal property, such as their family homes. Creditors can also choose to obtain bankruptcy orders against individual partners without winding up the partnership as a whole!

The best way to illustrate the draconian nature of partnership insolvency is to use a typical case as an example.

Let us say a partnership with three partners runs into trouble, with debts of £400,000. The partnership jointly owns property worth £100,000 and each partner owns his own home, valued at

£150,000. A creditor petitions to have the partnership wound up and a liquidator is appointed to dispose of all of the partnership assets. He would take his expenses and fees first, and then pay out a dividend to creditors.

Later on, creditors may petition to have each of the partners bankrupted. A trustee in bankruptcy would then be appointed in each case to dispose of the each partner's home.

The running order of this procedure could be random and arbitrary, at the whim of creditors. They could bankrupt one partner rather than another, or two of them, or all of them. Also, the creditors could choose to bankrupt just two of the three partners and sell their homes to clear the partnership debts. The two partners selected would have to bear the full consequences. If this occurred, then these two partners could pursue claims against the one remaining partner, in an attempt to recover some of their own losses.

A partnership can also bring a bankruptcy order against itself, but all of the partners must agree to this. If a partnership bankrupts itself, and if all of the partners agree, this can have the effect of bankrupting the partnership as a whole, as well as each partner individually. This is because a partnership has its own common debts, whereas each individual partner may have additional personal borrowing. Thus a partnership bankruptcy usually creates a series of bankruptcies. If any partner does not agree to the partnership being bankrupted as a whole, then any partner can bankrupt himself as an individual. He would then immediately cease to be a partner in the partnership and his trustee in bankruptcy would then look to the other partners for his share of any partnership assets.

It should be clear to readers from the above, and for many other reasons too complex to explain here, that business partnerships are potential nightmares when things go wrong. The law is very complex and usually has devastating effects on all of the partners. Given the above facts, business partnerships should be avoided, if at all possible.

Partnership law has similar effects in every country in the United Kingdom, although the above comments are based on the law in England and Wales.

6

Discharge from Bankruptcy

There are several types of discharge from bankruptcy. These are:

Discharge from a First Bankruptcy

An automatic discharge from a first bankruptcy is normally granted after three years. The discharge would only be suspended if the bankrupt had not co-operated with the proceedings or had broken the bankruptcy laws. If an official receiver or a trustee wishes to suspend a discharge and keep someone in bankruptcy, then he must make an application to the court, before the automatic discharge is due. The bankrupt would be informed of this application and it would then be the decision of the court, on hearing the evidence, to make such order as it thinks fit.

If a bankrupt brought the bankruptcy petition against himself and, in addition, had debts of less than £20,000, he would receive an automatic discharge after two years. If, however, a creditor brought a bankruptcy petition against someone owing less than £20,000, then an automatic discharge would not be granted until three years had passed.

No notification of discharge is sent to the bankrupt. A certificate of discharge may be obtained by writing to the clerk of the court where the bankruptcy order was made, on or after the appropriate anniversary, quoting the details of the bankruptcy. A certificate of discharge will then be supplied within a few weeks. It is useful to have this as proof of discharge, but discharge does not depend upon the obtaining of this certificate. A discharge releases a bankrupt from all of his debts, except for those associated with fraud. The position concerning fraud is draconian in the extreme, in that there would appear to be no release from such debts. I have no practical knowledge of any cases were creditors have continued to pursue debts associated with fraud after bankruptcy, but that they have the right to do so is clear from the law.

A discharged bankrupt is released from his debts and returned to normality, in a legal sense. In law, he can once again obtain credit and a mortgage and own property. In reality, the bankrupt's credit rating is likely to be affected by a bankruptcy order for up to fifteen years. Credit reference agencies keep bankruptcies recorded, on average, for around eight years. It is therefore obvious that there may well be difficulty in obtaining credit, even after discharge from bankruptcy.

Likewise, some banks will still be cautious about opening accounts for discharged bankrupts. Whilst preparing this book I wrote to the chairmen of several large banks and building societies, asking for their policies on such cases. Fairly woolly replies were received, but the general tenor was that they treat individual cases on their own merit. It has been my experience that most discharged bankrupts find it reasonably easy to obtain mortgages again. The experiences, however, that discharged bankrupts have in obtaining bank accounts are mixed. Some bank managers are helpful, others are not. The secret seems to be to try a number of banks, until one is found which is willing to help.

Discharge from Second Bankruptcies

An automatic discharge from a second bankruptcy may also be granted after three years. An automatic discharge, however, will not be granted where a second bankruptcy order has been made within 15 years of a person still being a bankrupt, ie within 15 years of being discharged from a first bankruptcy. In these cases, people will be held in their second bankruptcies for a minimum period of five years. The bankrupt should then make an application to the court for his discharge.

Suspended Discharges

In cases where the official receiver or trustee has succeeded in obtaining a court order denying the automatic discharge, an application must then be made to the court in order to obtain a discharge. It would be necessary for the bankrupt to show that they have dealt with the problems which caused the discharge to be suspended.

Annulment of Bankruptcy Order

If the money raised by the trustee, or by the bankrupt, is sufficient to pay all of the debts and costs associated with the bankruptcy (usually a huge amount), then the bankruptcy order may be annulled by the court. This immediately frees the person from bankruptcy and in a legal sense, it is as if the bankruptcy had never occurred. The occurrence of the original bankruptcy will still have been recorded by the credit reference agencies, so an annulment will not eradicate, by any means, all of the damage of such a bankruptcy.

7

Disputes with Trustees and Official Receivers

Many bankrupt people run into disputes with their trustees in bankruptcy and/or their official receivers and feel aggrieved by the actions of those in charge of their affairs. The bankrupt is always at a disadvantage in these disputes as official receivers and trustees have a legal authority to act in various matters.

In addition, it has been the universal experience of thousands of bankrupt people that obtaining any decent legal advice is extremely difficult and often very nearly impossible. All the odds are stacked against the bankrupt. The law offers the bankrupt few rights and few bankrupt people have funds to pay for legal advice. In any event, the majority of solicitors barely have a nodding acquaintance with bankruptcy law. It is also difficult to obtain legal aid in the majority of bankruptcy related actions.

From the years of experience the Bankruptcy Association has had in pursuing complaints against trustees and official receivers, the two main routes to take action are as follows:

Complaining to the Authorising Body

Every trustee in bankruptcy is an insolvency practitioner, author-ised by one of a number of authorising bodies. If a bankrupt feels he is being mistreated by his trustee, he may complain to the appropriate body, who will then investigate the complaint. Persistence is required when making these complaints, as the authorising bodies have a bias in favour of their members.

Complaints about official receivers may be made directly to Insolvency Service headquarters. The details of the authorising bodies of particular trustees may also be obtained from them. The contact addresses for readers in connection with this are:

The Inspector General of Bankruptcy and Agency Chief Executive
The Insolvency Service
PO Box 203
21 Bloomsbury Street
London
WC1B 3QW

Tel: 0171 6371110

Bankrupts in Northern Ireland should complain to:

The Official Receiver
The Insolvency Service
Department of Economic Development
8–14 Callender Street
Belfast
BT1 5DU

Tel: 01232 248885

Scottish bankrupts should refer to chapter 8 to read about the different position in Scotland.

Taking Direct Legal Action

Very few bankrupts are aware that they may make an application to the court concerning any action by their trustee about which they are aggrieved. It is worth quoting here section 303 subsection 1 of the Insolvency Act 1986, which reads as follows:

'If a bankrupt or any of his creditors or any other person is dissatisfied by any act, omission or decision of a trustee of the bankrupt's estate, he may apply to the court; and on such an application the court may confirm, reverse or modify any act or decision of the trustee, may give him directions or may make such other order as it thinks fit.'

This section is the single most powerful legal weapon which a bankrupt has at his disposal. An application to court under section 303 currently costs just ten pounds to make and requires the swearing of an affidavit, listing the areas of complaint, with supporting evidence.

One of our members, a bankrupt woman doctor, recently used this section with devastating legal effect against her trustee. Without any legal support whatsoever, she brought a series of complaints against him, succeeding with her applications on each occasion. Her trustee was furious over the matter, as he was not awarded costs in any of the actions.

Readers need to be aware that if they bring a court action against the trustee which the court considers to be spurious, or not justifiable, then there is a risk that the legal costs of the trustee may be awarded against the bankrupt. Bankrupts should be confident that their potential court actions are justified before bringing an application under section 303.

Obtaining Legal Support

I have already indicated the difficulties experienced by bankrupt people when trying to obtain decent legal advice. The number of specialist insolvency lawyers in the United Kingdom is very small and most of them are, in any case, creditor orientated, working on the side of the trustee in bankruptcy.

A list of all the specialist insolvency lawyers can be found in Chambers & Partners' Directory of the Legal Profession. The latest edition which I have to hand is for 1994–95 and is available for £19.95 from Chambers & Partners, 74 Long Lane, London EC1A 9ET. This may also be available in some reference libraries.

Over recent years the Bankruptcy Association has been very pleased to work with Carrick Read Insolvency, a specialist firm of insolvency lawyers. They have proved themselves more than happy to take the side of the bankrupt person, when appropriate, and they have been remarkably successful when acting for Bankruptcy

Association members. Carrick Read are highly recommended in the Chambers Directory, referred to above. I have no hesitation in seconding that commendation. They are superb lawyers but readers are reminded that, like all specialist legal advisers, their fees may be considerable, depending on the work and time involved. They will, however, quote a fixed fee for specific legal tasks. The contacts for Carrick Read at the time of writing are:

Hull:

Carrick Read Insolvency
Norwich House
Savile Street
Hull
HU1 3ES

Tel: 01482 211160
Contacts: Christopher Garwood
            Francesca Devine

Leeds:

Carrick Read Insolvency
Trafalgar House
29 Park Place
Leeds
LS1 2SP

Tel: 0113 2432911
Contact: Andrew Laycock

London:

Carrick Read Insolvency
Salisbury House
London Wall
London
EC2M 5PS

Tel: 0171 2165560
Contact: Stephen Baister

8

Differences in Scottish Bankruptcy Law

Scotland has its own distinctive bankruptcy laws, governed by the Bankruptcy (Scotland) Act 1985 (as amended). There is little point in this chapter in repeating the majority of matters which are common to other parts of the UK.

Therefore most of the advice given in earlier chapters may be assumed to apply to Scottish readers, with some very important exceptions, as explained below.

Terminology Differences

The term sequestration is often used in Scotland in place of the word bankruptcy. Both words have the same meaning. There are also other Scottish legal words and phrases used in place of their English equivalent. I do not propose to outline all of these here, as I feel sure that our well educated Scottish readers will be capable of carrying out the necessary translation themselves.

Creditor's Bankruptcy Petition

In Scotland a creditor can only bring a petition against a debtor for a debt of £1500 or more – not £750 as in England. By a peculiar quirk in the law, however, a creditor can issue a statutory demand (one of the prerequisites for bringing a bankruptcy petition) for a sum of £750. If that creditor can then find another creditor (or other creditors) to bring the total debt due to £1500, then they can join together and bring a bankruptcy petition based on the statutory demand for the smaller sum. I would like to know the Scottish logic behind this peculiar system!

Debtor's Bankruptcy Petition

The method in Scotland for a debtor to bring his own bankruptcy petition is much more complicated than in England, where a bankruptcy order will be granted on the production of the correct form and fee. In Scotland, a debtor can only bring a bankruptcy petition against himself in his Sheriff's Court if:

a) He has not been sequestrated in Scotland within the last five years

b) He has debts of at least £1500

and

c) He can show one of the following is true:

1) That he has failed to make payment to any creditor of any debt due under a court decree, and a charge for payment of that debt has expired, without payment having been made, or

2) That he has failed to make payment to any creditor of any debt due under a summary warrant for recovery of rates or taxes and fourteen days have elapsed since the date of any poinding to recover that debt, or

3) A decree of adjudication has been granted against him for any part of his estate, either for payment or in security, or

4) His effects have been sold under a decree for sequestration for rent, or

5) A receiving order has been made against him in England and Wales, or

6) A statutory demand has been served on him requiring him to

pay a sum claimed to be due or to find security for payment within three weeks and the debtor has failed to:

i) comply with that demand, or

ii) intimate to the creditor, by means of recorded delivery service, that he denies that the sum claimed is immediately payable, or

7) That he has been sequestrated or adjudged bankrupt in England, Wales or Northern Ireland, or

8) The debtor has signed a trust deed which has not become protected (see trust deeds below).

I could easily write a long essay here on these somewhat ludicrous requirements to bring a bankruptcy petition in Scotland, compared to the simple procedure elsewhere in the United Kingdom. Suffice it to say that the requirements to go bankrupt in Scotland were toughened up, by political intervention, to check an explosion of bankruptcies which had occurred as a result of earlier liberalisation of the legislation, during 1985.

Once the requirements have been met, then a petition can be brought in the Sheriff's court, on completion of the appropriate forms obtainable from the court and payment of a fee of £53 (as at 21 July 1995).

Accountant in Bankruptcy

The Accountant in Bankruptcy fulfils two roles: first, he is generally responsible for bankruptcy administration in Scotland, which would equate to the official receiver of an English region. Secondly, he also has a team of staff, based in Edinburgh, who will assist him in acting as trustee when he is appointed in bankruptcy cases where no other trustee is nominated. Similar to the official receiver in England, he will usually act in cases where there are few or no assets, but does not restrict his activities solely to these cases. Where he declines to have his staff administer cases, they are passed out to private trustees, who will act as his agents.

Choice of Trustee by Debtor

In Scotland (unlike elsewhere in the United Kingdom), it is possible, in certain instances, for the debtor to nominate his trustee in bankruptcy. If there are assets to pay for the fees of a private trustee, then a debtor may approach an insolvency practitioner and ask him for a letter accepting nomination as trustee in bankruptcy. If the proposed trustee agrees, then his letter is placed with the bankruptcy petition, on which he is named as interim trustee. If there are few or no assets, then this may still be done by negotiating a fee with the proposed trustee. There are differences in the personal character of various private trustees, so it may well have benefits to the debtor to be able to choose his own trustee where a good working relationship can be envisaged.

Home Visits

In Scotland, if the Accountant in Bankruptcy is acting as trustee in bankruptcy, then one of his staff will visit the bankrupt at his home after the bankruptcy order has been made, in order to interview him. This is rarely the case in the rest of the United Kingdom, where the interviews invariably take place at the local Official Receiver's office. The Accountant in Bankruptcy says his system is designed to be 'user friendly' – although in truth some people find this intimidating. A private trustee, if appointed, might also send his representative to visit the bankrupt at home, as occasionally happens in the rest of the United Kingdom.

Trust Deeds

Trust deeds are the Scottish equivalent of the individual voluntary arrangements (IVAs) to be found elsewhere in the UK and suffer from the same limitations as I highlighted within the IVA section. As a consequence of the Scottish restrictions on a debtor petitioning for his own bankruptcy, trust deeds may, however, be used as a means to an end, when no other remedy is available. I would therefore recommend that Scottish readers discuss the advantages and disadvantages of trust deeds versus bankruptcy with a skilled professional adviser, such as the ones referred to below, or with the Bankruptcy Association itself.

The Family Home

In Scotland, if a house is owned solely by the husband and is not in joint names, then the trustee in bankruptcy is entitled to all of the proceeds of any equity in the property. In England and Wales, a married woman would be entitled to a half share of the equity, even if the property was solely in the name of her husband. A married woman in Scotland is only entitled to a half share in the family home if it is jointly owned. This strikes me as being very unfair and is perhaps something that should be challenged in the European Courts one day.

Discharge from Bankruptcy

In Scotland, discharge from bankruptcy normally occurs after three years, but it can be suspended by the court for successive periods of two years if the bankrupt fails to co-operate with his trustee.

Recommended advisers in Scotland

The Bankruptcy Association has had a long-standing relationship with two professional advisers in Scotland, both of whom we hold in the highest regard. We would have have no hesitation in recommending readers to seek advice from either of these gentlemen.

The insolvency practitioner we recommend is Alan O'Boyle, of Walkers, Chartered Accountants, 82 Mitchell Street, Glasgow G1 3PX. Tel: 0141 2484211. Alan O'Boyle accepts appointments to act as trustee and will advise in general insolvency procedures in Scotland.

The solicitor we recommend is Fergus Ewing of Ewing & Co, Solicitors, 52 Queen's Drive, Glasgow G42 8DD. Tel: 0141 423 1765. Fergus is an excellent, debtor friendly, Glasgow solicitor.

Making Complaints in Scotland

There is a system, peculiar to Scotland, whereby any bankrupt can complain about any matter appertaining to his bankruptcy, direct to the Sheriff of the court where the order was made. In addition a bankrupt may also complain direct to:

The Accountant in Bankruptcy
Haymarket House
7 Clifton Terrace
Edinburgh
EH12 5DR

Tel: 0131 3134549

A bankrupt may also complain to the authorising body of any private trustee who may have been appointed. The names and addresses of the authorising bodies may be obtained from the Accountant in Bankruptcy.

In general terms therefore, it is easier to air complaints in Scotland than elsewhere.

Conclusion

It is not possible in this, a layman's guide to Scottish bankruptcy law, to cross every t and dot every i in the differences in the law throughout the UK. Bankruptcy law is very complex technical legislation and there may be other differences to those outlined above. I have endeavoured to cover the main differences. I have also had this chapter checked by Alan O'Boyle, the very experienced Scottish insolvency practitioner, referred to above.

9

The Psychological Trauma of Bankruptcy

What is known as 'bankruptcy neurosis,' the breakdown of judgement as bankruptcy approaches, has long been acknowledged. Through my work with the Bankruptcy Association, I long ago also identified the 'bankruptcy illness' which refers to the longer term psychological effects of bankruptcy experienced by many people. In some cases, this also results in physical illness. I recently spoke to a doctor practising in a small Welsh village, who himself was burdened with debt problems. He estimated that half of the medical problems of his patients were debt related. Another doctor from Liverpool, who had gone bankrupt as a result of modernising his practice, was so concerned about the debt worries of his patients that he held a special surgery on Saturdays, simply to deal with these problems.

The psychological effect of bankruptcy on each individual varies enormously, depending on their personalities and individual circumstances. A few, just a few, ride out a bankruptcy quite well and recover psychologically fairly quickly. For people living in rented accommodation, who are perhaps unemployed and saddled with debts, a bankruptcy might bring a blessed relief from creditor pressure.

For most people in business, and the majority of bankruptcies in the United Kingdom are business bankruptcies, bankruptcy can bring with it an awful personal trauma too. Bankrupts have usually lost their status and their livelihood, and in many cases will also lose their homes. If they have the responsibilities of a family, the psychological impact can be devastating.

Many bankrupts are highly educated, professional people. The sudden switch from being a respected member of the community to being just a bankruptcy number in the official receiver's office can have a devastating impact on the bankrupt's confidence and ability to cope with life in the future. These difficulties are compounded by the restrictions which bankruptcy imposes on people until, and often beyond, their discharge.

I have no magical solution to offer those suffering the trauma of bankruptcy. I can only hope it will help such people to soldier on by reading here that their own feelings are shared by many others. Becoming members of the Bankruptcy Association would help such people too, as they may then meet others in the same position and receive the Association's newsletters and other literature. The address of the Association can be found in chapter 11.

10

Pulling the Plug on a Limited Company

This chapter deals briefly with the position regarding limited companies which run into financial problems, as distinct from individuals, sole traders or partnerships, excepting that partnerships in England and Wales can be wound up as if they were limited companies in certain circumstances (see chapter 5). Except for very minor differences in procedures, the law is almost identical in England, Wales, Scotland and Northern Ireland in so far as the treatment of limited companies is concerned. Although this chapter is based on the law in England, it is generally applicable throughout the United Kingdom.

Directors of limited companies should remember that except when a company is forcibly wound up, or put into receivership, then the fees need to be found, and usually paid up front, to follow voluntary winding up procedures. These procedures can be expensive, often running into thousands of pounds.

The concept of limited liability is more than one hundred years old and was introduced to provide protection for those in business, at a time of rapid commercial expansion, during the nineteenth century. It was designed to remove some of the risks involved from individual businessmen and to spread that risk amongst creditors. The habit of banks, landlords and others, however, in seeking personal guarantees from directors has increasingly eroded the concept of limited liability. In addition, the Insolvency Act 1986 introduced 'wrongful trading' provisions. Directors, or even 'shadow' directors, of a company, who are believed to have acted irresponsibly may now be, and have been, made liable in whole, or in part, for the debts of a limited company.

There are currently six major methods to deal with insolvent companies. These are:

1) Company voluntary arrangements
2) Administration orders
3) Receivership
4) Members' voluntary winding up
5) Creditors' voluntary winding up
6) Winding up by the court

The legal term 'winding up' is invariably referred to, both inside and outside of the insolvency profession, as 'liquidation'. For the purposes of this chapter therefore, the terms liquidation and winding up have the same meaning.

Company Voluntary Arrangements

One method of dealing with insolvency is a company voluntary arrangement. A company director may apply for a voluntary arrangement for his company at anytime. A voluntary arrangement is a proposal put to creditors, to dispose of stock and assets and/or make a contribution from future earnings, to pay out a dividend to creditors, in full settlement of a company's debts. It requires the agreement of 75 per cent of unsecured creditors by money value, to accept such a proposal, which then becomes binding on all unsecured creditors.

In practice, these arrangements for limited companies are not working out very well, for a number of reasons. First, it is costly to set up an arrangement for a company (several thousand pounds in most cases). Secondly, a company's creditor and debtor position is usually rapidly changing and it is difficult to forecast future cashflow. Thirdly, banks who hold securities are usually keen to enforce those securities.

Administration Orders

The administration order procedure allows a company's directors, or its creditors, to apply to the Court to have an administrator take over the running of a company's affairs.

An administration order can best be described as a half-way house between solvency and receivership. The idea behind the appointment of an administrator is that he has wider and more flexible powers to run a company as a going concern, than a receiver. He will, hopefully, be able to pull the company through its difficulties.

In practice, many administration orders have merely been the means of realising assets, before formal liquidation has taken place. In a few special cases, such as football clubs, administration orders have worked well. In many other cases, however, they have proved an unnecessary and expensive formality. They have not generally proved very practical.

Receivership

The various types of receivership are too complex to outline in detail. Suffice it to say that the appointment of a receiver is generally at the instigation of a major creditor (more often than not the bank). Quite often a bank will have an automatic power to appoint a receiver, even without applying to the court, if they follow specified procedures. By such methods the control of businesses can be torn from the control of their directors, and sold off, sometimes within hours, to their competitors. There are grave concerns about these procedures.

Receivership usually signals the quick and sudden death knell for a company, resulting fairly quickly in the closing of its operations, the dismissal of all staff, and the rapid sale and disposal of the company or its assets.

Members' Voluntary Winding Up

A members liquidation can take place when, although a company is unable to pay its debts on time, it can do so within a period of twelve months.

The directors swear out a 'statutory declaration of solvency' and the shareholders may then appoint their own liquidator to deal with the company's affairs.

Creditors' Voluntary Winding Up

In a creditors' voluntary liquidation, the shareholders pass a resolution for the winding up of a company and then appoint a liquidator of their choice, to be the liquidator of the company. A meeting of the company's creditors then takes place, who may approve of the appointed liquidator, or alternatively, appoint one of their own choice.

Winding Up by the Court

Any creditor of a company with an overdue debt of £750, or a combination of creditors owed that amount or more, may issue a formal demand for repayment. This may simply be by letter. On the basis of that demand, an application may be made to have the company put into liquidation, if the debt has not been paid within three weeks. There is no need to have an unsatisfied judgement debt, before such a petition may be issued.

This leaves companies very exposed to their unsecured creditors, who can quickly and easily bring a company's operations to a halt.

When a company is wound up in this way, by order of the court, then the official receiver is automatically appointed liquidator. Later, if the company has sufficient assets, the official receiver will hold a meeting of creditors to appoint an insolvency practitioner to take over as liquidator.

Directors of companies wound up by the Court will face personal examination by the official receiver about the causes of the business failure. Winding up by the Court is, therefore, generally seen as the most serious form of liquidation, because of the implication that the directors may have acted irresponsibly, by not implementing an alternative procedure, before the creditors moved to wind up the company.

Other Points

Whichever of these routes is taken by a company in trouble, the receiver or liquidator is obliged to report on the conduct of the directors of the company to the Department of Trade and Industry. The DTI may use these reports to bring prosecutions under the Company Directors Disqualification Act 1986. This enables the court to disqualify irresponsible directors from taking part in the future management of another business, for prescribed periods.

A register of disqualifications is maintained from which information is obtained by credit reference agencies, who, in turn, transmit this information to their users.

Finally, directors of insolvent limited companies sometimes find themselves personally liable for borrowings from the company, such as director loan accounts, and certain tax debts. Directors of limited companies in trouble should make sure they take care not to get trapped in this way, by taking the appropriate advice.

11

The Bankruptcy Association

I founded the Bankruptcy Association of Great Britain and Ireland in March 1983 as a result of the second horrendous bankruptcy of my eldest brother, Jim. In the epilogue which follows this chapter, I explain how powerfully my brother's bankruptcy affected me. For most people, going bankrupt is a very emotional experience

I knew there must be other people in a similar position who needed help. I was aware, from trying to help Jim, of the lack of specialist advice available. My brother felt great anger against the bankruptcy machine and I simply had to do something to help him, and others like him. Some people seek out causes and crusades. In my case, the cause was simply thrust upon me. Once I started down what I knew would be a long and difficult path (and so it proved), I also knew that there would be no turning back.

The Association was a small scale affair at first which I ran, with the help of others, as a voluntary organisation between 1983 and 1989, by which time membership had grown to around 600. I made my living as a business writer during much of this period, writing advice articles for the business and trade press. I also honed up my knowledge of bankruptcy law and I wrote my first book: 'What to do when someone has debt problems' which was published in 1985.

I also met many real flesh and blood bankrupt people and quickly discovered that the majority of them were fine and honourable men and women, who had been unfortunate in business. I also learned that the causes of each bankruptcy are as complex and varied as people themselves.

There have been times that pursuing this cause has brought me to my knees, because of the many difficulties and problems I have had to overcome. It was always the knowledge that real people needed the Bankruptcy Association's help which kept me going. In the early years of my work I was dubbed in the press as a 'lone crusader.' I have, indeed, felt very alone at times, but no more so than the majority of bankrupt people who are often deserted by family and friends in their time of need.

During the course of 1989, economic disaster overtook Britain. The property market collapsed and the banks began to pull the plug from under thousands of businesses, because of the decline in the value of their securities.

Personal bankruptcies rose from a few thousand a year to tens of thousands, peaking at more than 32,000 during 1993. During this incredible period membership of our Association climbed from a few hundred to nearly three thousand. The work took over my life completely. In addition, in 1990, Gill Hankey, a lady who lost her business early in the slump, volunteered to help me run the Association. We have continued to work together full-time as a team since then.

This book is the replacement for 'Bankruptcy – The Reality and the Law,' an advice book I wrote and which the Bankruptcy Association published early in 1992. 'Bankruptcy – The Reality and the Law' ran to two editions and sold 10,000 copies. 'Bankruptcy Explained' updates my views on bankruptcy law and is more extensive in its coverage of the law. The incredible story of the last five years of the Bankruptcy Association is outlined in my book: 'Boom to Bust – The Great 1990s Slump,' which the Bankruptcy Association published in November 1994.

At the time of writing there is a decline in the number of personal bankruptcies to around two thirds of the peak figure. It is expected, however, that there will be about 20,000 bankruptcies per annum until the end of this century and probably beyond.

The Bankruptcy Association has, over the past few years,

developed the services offered to members. Membership of the Association currently costs £15 per year. This gives members access to our telephone advice line, as well as our regular newsletters. We also hold meetings for Association members, we give personal consultations and offer a very popular negotiating service. The main achievement of the Bankruptcy Association, however, is simply being here, day by day, month by month, year by year, as an independent organisation working tirelessly on behalf of its members. We are friendly faces for bankrupt people to turn to, in an otherwise unfriendly world. We understand full well the indignities and humiliations which bankrupt people experience. The Bankruptcy Association holds out a hand of friendship to its members and provides them with support founded on knowledge and experience gained over more than a decade.

More details about the Association may be obtained by writing to The Bankruptcy Association, FREEPOST, 4 Johnson Close, Lancaster LA1 1BR. The telephone number of the Association is 01524 64305.

Epilogue: Over the Sea to Skye

Speed, bonny boat, like a bird on the wing
Onwards the sailors cry:
Carry the lad that's born to be King
Over the sea to Skye.

'Which circus is this then?' joked the Skye ferry skipper as an odd assortment of jeeps, beaten up vans, trucks and assorted caravans and trailers rolled aboard the ferry at the Kyle of Lochalsh to cross the narrow strip of water to the Isle of Skye, early in 1983.

'It's Big Jim McQueen's circus', quipped back Steve Brooks, Big Jim's brother in law. Steve had just endured the three day trip from Lancaster to the Kyle of Lochalsh, forming part of my bankrupt brother's convoy of retreat from Lancaster to a new life in Skye.

I had watched the convoy leave my home town of Lancaster with great regret and a sense of overwhelming sadness. An important chapter in my life was over. I did not know it then, but I was to rarely see my eldest brother again before his untimely death. He died in Edinburgh in 1989, just 48 years old, after a heart operation failed.

Although Big Jim's life was a relatively short one, he lived a life packed with drama. He endured two bankruptcies and had more adventures than ten more ordinary men would have had living their lives to the full three score years and ten. He was a born adventurer and a dreamer, a man unafraid to climb mountains.

The story of the convoy to Skye is just a titbit out of Big Jim's many adventures. Although my instincts urged me to go on that journey, I was unable to because of family commitments. I am fortunate, however, in knowing virtually every detail about the trip from the numerous family members and others who did take part. In particular, my brother in law, Steve Brooks, told me the yarn several times in a fashion that beautifully combined the pathos, humour and magic of the grand journey.

Big Jim led the convoy up the M6 from Lancaster, towing a huge mobile home on the back of a specially built trailer, pulled by an ex US army truck. By the time they reached Carlisle the odd assortment of vehicles had attracted the attention of the police. Before long they were being shadowed by two police cars!

On crossing the border into Scotland a police helicopter, complete with TV camera, joined in the monitoring operation and the English police cars were replaced by two from Scotland. These kept the convoy company until it leagued for the first night. Progress was slow as they only averaged 20 mph on the 450 mile journey because of the weight of gear being carried and towed, and because of a series of breakdowns and punctures which plagued the assorted vehicles and trailers.

Big Jim was in a bad mood and was extremely tetchy. That was hardly surprising as he had suffered two heart attacks after his second bankruptcy in 1978, and had just been evicted from his home. He had a wife and five grown up children to worry about, as well as a three year old son and a two year old daughter with a heart defect. He tended to mellow in an evening over a hefty ration of Scotch whisky, his only remaining prop, having given up smoking after the heart attacks.

Searching for spares for a damaged trailer they ended up spending the first night in a scrap yard near Glasgow! They were unprepared for a night on the road as the plan had been to reach Skye on the first day. A nightmare ensued as the motley crew fought over food rations, bedding and cans of beer!

Somehow they survived that first night, repaired the damaged trailer, and the convoy set off again in the morning. By mid afternoon they were high up on the Pass of Glencoe, far from civilisation, when a major fault developed on the US truck bringing the whole convoy to a halt again. It looked like curtains for the whole adventure, as it was inconceivable that they would be able to obtain the specialist spares needed for an ex US army truck anywhere in Scotland – never mind high in the Pass of Glencoe!

Big Jim's temper flared and the morale of the adventurers

reached an all time low as they contemplated their bleak prospects, high in the mountains. My youngest brother, William and Steve Brooks set off in a jeep, in a forlorn attempt to find spares for the truck. They drove several miles down the steep road out of the pass and stopped at the first garage. By some miracle of fate it was the only garage in Scotland that had spares for those particular vehicles!

A few hours later and the convoy was able to continue its journey, although they had to spend another night, starving, cold and miserable, camped out in a lay by.

After more breakdowns and punctures, they finally rolled aboard the ferry at the Kyle of Lochalsh, late in the afternoon of the third day. The mountains of Skye, shrouded in mist as usual, beckoned them on. Morale rose as the group contemplated the fact that their nightmare trip was nearly over. All that remained was a fifty mile trip up the island to their resting place at Monkstadt steadings, a piece of land purchased by one of Jim's sons. It lay just beyond the small port and fishing village of Uig, in the far North of Skye.

Unknown to them, the real drama of the journey had not yet begun. As the convoy rolled across Skye, Big Jim began to worry about the huge trailer carrying his mobile home. The road from Uig to Monkstadt was only single track, with few passing places, and there was a terrifying hair pin bend to negotiate around the side of a steep mountain. Coaches negotiating the bend had to carry out tricky manoeuvres to get around safely. For any vehicle failing to negotiate the bend safely, the consequence would be fatal, as there was a sheer drop of several hundred feet down into the bay.

His nagging doubts soon turned into a real fear that the bend was too tight to negotiate. When the convoy stopped in Uig, he sent out a scouting party to see if they could reach Monkstadt by the only alternative route. This involved doing a circular tour to the north of the island. The scouting party returned an hour later to say that the road was too narrow and that there were too many obstacles which could snag the trailer.

Big Jim was now a very worried man indeed. He was convinced that the hairpin bend could not be negotiated. Once again the whole enterprise faced a doom laden end. To add to his problems a full scale gale, common to Skye, was beginning to blow up.

He left his son Jamie and Steve Brooks in the truck towing the mobile home, instructing them to wait at the foot of the mountain whilst he reconnoitred the bend. He also told them he would signal them as to whether it was safe for them to try and negotiate it. He took out his tape and carefully measured the length of the truck and the trailer and then set off up the road to the bend. He measured the traverse of the bend, and after making some exact mathematical calculations, he worked out that there was not the slightest chance that the truck and the trailer could safely get around it.

In his haste and concern, however, Big Jim had not left very clear instructions as to the nature of the signal he would make to his son, waiting in the truck. Jim simply stood on the side of the mountain and began waving his arms in what he believed was a clear signal to his son, instructing him to remain where he was.

The signal was completely misread! His son Jamie took the signal to mean that it was safe to take the bend and he gunned up the truck engine and headed up the mountainside like a bat out of hell. It was at this point – too late – that Steve Brooks, sitting in the passenger seat of the truck, began to have second thoughts about the meaning of Big Jim's signal. Steve's rising fear heightened to one of pure terror as they approached the bend.

Jamie had a large streak of his father's character in him, and he hit the bend, unperturbed, on full throttle. As they hurtled into it Steve knew he was about to die and looked in horror at the sheer drop that awaited them.

Two miracles then followed in quick succession. The first was that Big Jim did not have another heart attack and die on the spot, as he prepared himself for the imminent death of the two lunatics in the truck. He screamed himself to exhaustion trying to warn them to stop.

Then the second miracle happened. They made it round the bend. Just! One of the back wheels of the trailer found itself in mid air, but somehow the truck and the trailer lurched round the bend to safety.

After that episode, arriving at the entrance to the road to Monkstadt, into the teeth of a howling gale was small beer. Quietly, noticed only by Steve Brooks out of the corner of his eye, Big Jim kissed the ground and said a short, silent prayer.

Quickly rising to his feet, he led the convoy up the mile long unmade road. This took another hour and by now it was dark. In pouring rain, and against howling winds, they widened a gap in a stone wall to get through to their little piece of Scotland. Finally, they roped everything down to prevent their entire expedition from being blown into eternity.

By midnight they had finished and they all collapsed wet and exhausted, into an uncomfortable sleep. They had made it to the end of another typical Big Jim adventure!

This story paints well the character of the man whose experiences were to lead me into my own amazing adventures within the strange world of bankruptcy, and along a winding road of discovery that seemingly has no end.

Big Jim was a big man with a big heart. He was a man I thought could never die. When I saw him dead in his coffin some years later – a bearded, giant of a man – he looked like some great warrior king who had endured a thousand storms and fought a hundred battles.

OTHER PUBLICATIONS OF THE BANKRUPTCY ASSOCIATION

BOOM TO BUST
The Great 1990s Slump

by John McQueen

John McQueen, founder of the Bankruptcy Association of Great Britain and Ireland, lived through the great slump of the 1990s in a special way. He was uniquely placed in the centre of it. In this bulldozer of a book, John McQueen turns a machine gun on the bankruptcy laws in the United Kingdom, as well as detailing the moving story of human suffering he lived through. He exposes, in the passing, many other flaws in the political and legal systems. He also argues that we have a difficult time ahead putting the country to rights. This book makes a social statement of immense importance.

Some review comments:

'This short, choleric, straight-from-the shoulder polemic asserts the iniquities of bankruptcy law as reflected in the experiences of encountering and advising those who found themselves "on the rocks," and of lobbying the authorities for more humane treatment of the afflicted.'

– The Business Economist

'The author demonstrates that all bankrupts, whatever the level of blame, receive harsh treatment from our society.'

– International Small Business Journal

Boom to Bust is available at the published price of £12.95 from bookshops or by return of post from:

> The Bankruptcy Association
> FREEPOST
> 4 Johnson Close
> Lancaster
> LA1 1BR